Find It: Hawai'i' Snorkeling Edition
A Field Notebook for the Young Explorer

Copyright © 2013 Revised 2017
By Kendall Roberg

Photography by: Kendall Roberg
Artistic Direction & Dive Support
by: Shelley Roberg

ISBN-10: 1482519372
ISBN-13: 978-1482519372

Step 1
Put on your mask, snorkel, and fins then start exploring!

Step 2
When an animal has been sighted, record your findings on the corresponding page.

Step 3
Calculate your point total on the last page to determine your Explorer Level.

Yellow Tang *Zebrasoma flavescens*

You can find this popular Hawaiian reef fish in shallow rocky areas where they graze on algae and marine plants. The white spine at the base of the tail can be extended for defense.

Sighting Date:	Sighting Location:

Observations:

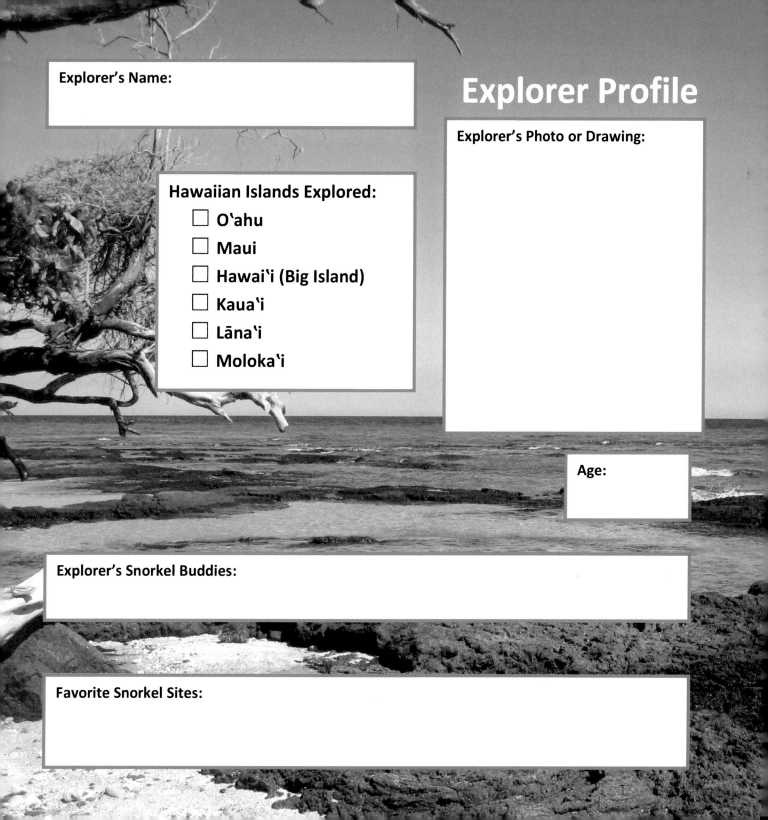

Explorer Profile

Explorer's Name:

Explorer's Photo or Drawing:

Hawaiian Islands Explored:
- ☐ Oʻahu
- ☐ Maui
- ☐ Hawaiʻi (Big Island)
- ☐ Kauaʻi
- ☐ Lānaʻi
- ☐ Molokaʻi

Age:

Explorer's Snorkel Buddies:

Favorite Snorkel Sites:

Yellow Tang

Zebrasoma flavescens

You can find this popular Hawaiian reef fish in shallow rocky areas where they graze on algae and marine plants. The white spine at the base of the tail can be extended for defense.

Sighting Date:

Sighting Location:

Observations:

Sergeant Damselfish

Abudefduf vaigiensis

You can find these common damselfish swimming all over the reef but you might notice they stay close to their "home" coral patch. These fish grow up to eight inches in length but are usually smaller.

Sighting Date:

Sighting Location:

Observations:

Threadfin Butterflyfish

Chaetodon auriga

This fish is named for the thin threadlike extension coming off the end of its dorsal fin (near the black spot). You can find it swimming over the sand near the reef.

Sighting Date:

Sighting Location:

Observations:

Banded Urchin

Echinothrix calamaris

Hopefully you do not find one these sea urchins by accident. Their long spines are needle sharp and can break off under your skin. Carefully look for them on the top of the reef.

Sighting Date:

Sighting Location:

Observations:

Hawaiian Whitespotted Toby

Canthigaster jactator

These small fish are part of the puffer family and are only found in Hawai'i'. They are fun to watch swim as they bend their tails to maneuver like tiny submarines. Find them at almost every snorkel site.

Sighting Date:

Sighting Location:

Observations:

Arc-Eye Hawkfish

Paracirrhites arcatus

Find this fish perched on the top of corals or rocks using its modified pectoral fins that work like small hands which allow for perching. This fish is also found in a darker color, but always features arcs around its eyes.

Sighting Date:

Sighting Location:

Observations:

Square-Spot Goatfish *Mulloidichthys flavolineatus*

Find these goatfish resting in groups on the sand or schooling around the reef. Anytime these fish are searching for food, mostly at night, they feature a penny-sized black square shaped spot on their sides.

Sighting Date:

Sighting Location:

Observations:

Convict Tang

Acanthurus triostegus

Find the babies of this species (about the size of a quarter) in tide pools or the much larger adults in rocky shallow areas.
The strips on this fish make it easy to identify.

Sighting Date:

Sighting Location:

Observations:

Raccoon Butterflyfish
Chaetodon lunula

The black mask across the face of this fish reminds many people of raccoons. The black spot near the base of the tail helps confuse predators. If you are lucky, you will find these fish drifting in a large group together.

Sighting Date:

Sighting Location:

Observations:

Hawaiian Dascyllus

Dascyllus albisella

These fish can often be found hovering around isolated coral heads in otherwise sandy areas. Young dascyllus are black with a central white spot while the adults look like those in the photo below.

Sighting Date:

Sighting Location:

Observations:

Fourspot Butterflyfish

Chaetodon quadrimaculatus

Each side of these fish feature two bright white spots. If you count the spots on *both* sides of these fish, there are a total of four. Like many butterflyfish, these are usually found in pairs.

Sighting Date:

Sighting Location:

Observations:

Saddle Wrasse

Thalassoma duperrey

The saddle wrasse is a wonderful fish to observe as it gracefully glides through the water. You can find them in rocky areas and identify them by the reddish brown "saddle" just behind their head.

Sighting Date:

Sighting Location:

Observations:

Humuhumu Triggerfish

Rhinecanthus aculeatus

This triggerfish is the Hawaiian state fish and can be found in the shallows digging under rocks and in the sand for small crabs and crustaceans to eat. This fishes full name is humuhumu-nukunuku-ā-pua'a.

Sighting Date:

Sighting Location:

Observations:

Spotted Boxfish

Ostracion meleagris

Find these colorful fish with boxlike bodies wandering over the coral reef. Only the males have the bright bluish-purple and gold coloration. The females are black with white spots (bottom left).

Sighting Date:

Sighting Location:

Observations:

Bluespotted Cornetfish

Fistularia commersonii

These long tube-like fish grow to over 4 feet long. Find them swimming smoothly over the bottom where they may be showing their light blue-gray coloration or their darker banded hunting colors.

Sighting Date:

Sighting Location:

Observations:

Green Sea Turtle   *Chelonia mydas*

Seeing a turtle while snorkeling is always a highlight. Find these fascinating creatures resting under ledges on the reef or swimming gracefully around the reef. Touching or chasing a sea turtle is illegal. Observe them calmly and they will usually stay with you and allow you to witness their interesting behaviors.

Sighting Date:

Sighting Location:

Observations:

Red Pencil Urchin
Heterocentrotus mammillatus

You can find the red pencil urchin in rocky areas and between coral heads on the reef. They are most active at night when they move around to feed on algae.

Sighting Date:

Sighting Location:

Observations:

Moorish Idol
Zanclus cornutus

The beautiful Moorish Idol can be found in shallow, calm water and features a long nose and an extra long trailing dorsal fin. These unique fish are always a treat to find while snorkeling.

Sighting Date:

Sighting Location:

Observations:

Longnose Butterflyfish

Forcipiger flavissimus

This fish can be found swimming in deeper areas and often upside down as it picks small prey off the ceilings of caves and ledges. Its long precise mouth allows it to be a picky eater.

Sighting Date:

Sighting Location:

Observations:

Bullethead Parrotfish   *Chlorurus spilurus*

Parrotfish use their beaks to scrape the coral. Dip down underwater and listen to the sound of their beaks in action. You may also notice a white stream of sand exiting the fish. Parrotfish produce much of Hawai'i's sand.

Sighting Date:

Sighting Location:

Observations:

Achilles Tang

Acanthurus achilles

These beautiful fish like the surge zone (where the waves crash onto the reef and the rocks). They swim quickly through the turbulent water and feed on algae growing on rocks and rubble.

Sighting Date:

Sighting Location:

Observations:

Stars and Stripes Puffer

Arothron hispidus

Find this football sized puffer swimming over the sand at beaches near popular resorts. These fish are full of curiosity and use their sharp beak-like teeth to crunch through anything edible.

Sighting Date:

Sighting Location:

Observations:

Bluefin Trevally

Caranx melampygus

If you spend enough time snorkeling in Hawai'i' you will eventually spot this beautiful predator. These fast and dedicated hunters can be observed searching the reef for unsuspecting prey.

Sighting Date:

Sighting Location:

Observations:

Snowflake Moray Eel

Echidna nebulosa

The Snowflake Moray Eel is one of the few eels that swim out in the open during the day. You can also occasionally find smaller Snowflake Moray Eels searching tide pools for small crabs.

Sighting Date:

Sighting Location:

Observations:

Great Barracuda

Sphyraena barracuda

These fish can grow up to six feet in length and are usually seen in the early morning or late afternoon. These are one of only a few fish who will make, and keep, eye contact with you. They are an intelligent fish.

Sighting Date:

Sighting Location:

Observations:

Pacific Trumpetfish

Aulostomus chinensis

The yellow morph of the trumpetfish is far less common than the normal dark coloration with light stripes and spots near the tail. This coloration is sometimes used to blend in with other yellow fishes.

Sighting Date:

Sighting Location:

Observations:

Day Octopus

Octopus cyanea

The day octopus is a master of camouflage and is usually overlooked by snorkelers as it perfectly matches the shape and color of the objects around it. If you spot one, stay still and the octopus will usually resume its activities.

Sighting Date:

Sighting Location:

Observations:

Bandit Angelfish

Apolemichthys arcuatus

Snorkelers in Kauai have the best chance of spotting this rare fish. These fish are not shy and will swim out in the open away from the reef and sometimes right over to snorkelers and divers.

Sighting Date:

Sighting Location:

Observations:

Cushion Star

Culcita novaeguineae

Sometimes called Mermaid Pillows, these plump creatures are part of the starfish family. They are usually found in deeper water on or near the base of the reef.

Sighting Date:

Sighting Location:

Observations:

Saddleback Butterflyfish

Chaetodon ephippium

Sightings of these fish are not common. They seem to prefer areas with healthy coral reefs. These fish are almost always found in pairs and move steadily over large areas of the reef.

Sighting Date:

Sighting Location:

Observations:

Hawaiian Monk Seal

Monachus schauinslandi

Hawaiian Monk Seals are one of the rarest marine mammals in the world. If you are lucky enough to see one, observe from a distance. These seals dive deep below the surface while hunting for food.

Sighting Date:

Sighting Location:

Observations:

Hawaiian Cleaner Wrasse   *Labroides phthirophagus*

These hardworking fish swim up and down to advertise their services. At their cleaning stations, they eat parasites and dead tissue off other fish. The larger filefish below is having his eye cleaned.

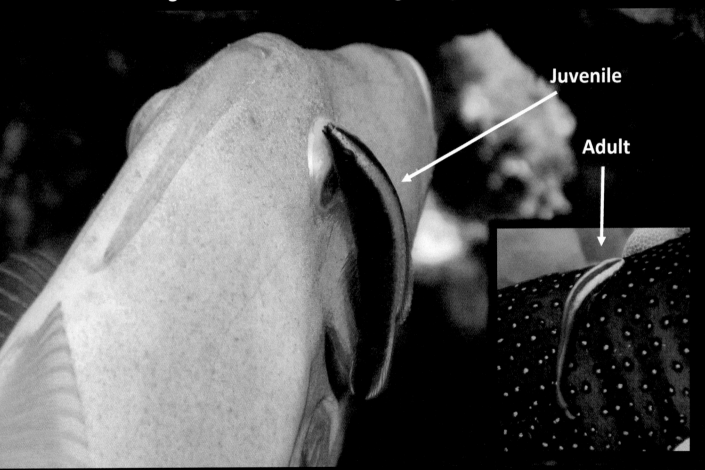

Juvenile

Adult

Sighting Date:

Sighting Location:

Observations:

Whitetip Reef Shark

Triaenodon obesus

Sharks are not a commonly seen sight while snorkeling in Hawai'i. If you do see one, it is likely this species. They are usually found resting on the bottom or swimming above the reef. These sharks are shy and not dangerous when left alone. Just observe them or calmly swim away.

Sighting Date:

Sighting Location:

Observations:

Potter's Angelfish

Centropyge potteri

Potter's Angelfish are difficult to find while snorkeling. Look for them in areas where the reef drops off. They weave gracefully through holes in the reef and are quite shy. They usually live in pairs or small

Sighting Date:

Sighting Location:

Observations:

Explorer Level

10 Points Each

- Yellow Tang
- Sergeant Damselfish
- Threadfin Butterflyfish
- Banded Urchin
- Hawaiian Whitespotted Toby
- Arc-Eye Hawkfish
- Square-Spot Goatfish
- Convict Tang
- Raccoon Butterflyfish
- Hawaiian Dascyllus
- Fourspot Butterflyfish
- Saddle Wrasse

20 Points Each

- Humuhumu Triggerfish
- Spotted Boxfish
- Bluespotted Cornetfish
- Green Sea Turtle
- Red Pencil Urchin
- Moorish Idol
- Longnose Butterflyfish
- Bullethead Parrotfish
- Achilles Tang
- Stars and Stripes Puffer
- Bluefin Trevally
- Snowflake Moray Eel

30 Points Each

- Great Barracuda
- Pacific Trumpetfish
- Day Octopus
- Bandit Angelfish
- Cushion Star
- Saddleback Butterflyfish
- Hawaiian Monk Seal
- Hawaiian Cleaner Wrasse
- Whitetip Reef Shark
- Potter's Angelfish

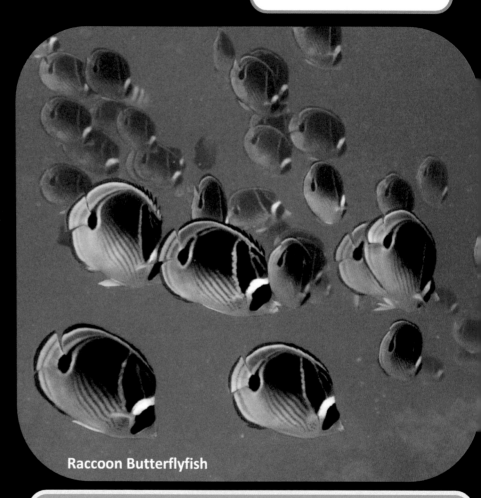

Raccoon Butterflyfish

Beginner	Intermediate	Expert
Less Than 100 Points	100 to 250 Points	More Than 250 Points

For kid friendly YouTube videos about Hawaiian sea creatures, visit the URL below or scan the QR code.

goo.gl/1uGiS0

About the Author & Photographer

Kendall Roberg has a passion for fish that draws him to the ocean to watch, learn from, and photograph Hawai'i's wonderful sea creatures. He loves sharing his passion with others and hopes this book will inspire young explorers to enjoy and respect the ocean's creatures.

The author would like to thank his amazing wife Shelley, Scuba Shack in Maui, and John Hoover (author of the best Hawaiian fish book ever written). Finally, thank you to Katherine Baker for editing.

Made in the USA
San Bernardino, CA
08 February 2020